PLEASANT HILL

A Giraffe Grows Up

by _____ rville

illustrated by Michael Denman and William J. Huiett

To my mother, Carol, the giraffe's biggest fan—Amanda.

Special thanks to our advisers for their expertise:

Zoological Society of San Diego
San Diego Zoo
San Diego, California

Susan Kesselring, M.A., Literacy Educator
Rosemount–Apple Valley–Eagan (Minnesota) School District

Editor: Christianne Jones
Designers: Angela Kilmer and Abbey Fitzgerald
Page Production: Melissa Kes
Art Director: Nathan Gassman
The illustrations in this book were created with acrylic.

Picture Window Books
5115 Excelsior Boulevard, Suite 232
Minneapolis, MN 55416
877-845-8392
www.picturewindowbooks.com

Printed in the United States of America.

Library of Congress Cataloging-in-Publication Data
Doering Tourville, Amanda, 1980-
A giraffe grows up / by Amanda Doering Tourville ;
illustrated by Michael Denman & William J. Huiett.
p. cm. — (Wild animals)
Includes bibliographical references and index.
ISBN-13: 978-1-4048-3158-2 (library binding)
ISBN-10: 1-4048-3158-4 (library binding)
ISBN-13: 978-1-4048-3565-8 (paperback)
ISBN-10: 1-4048-3565-2 (paperback)
1. Giraffe—Infancy—Juvenile literature. 2. Giraffe—Development—
Juvenile literature. I. Denman, Michael, ill. II. Huiett, William J., 1943- ill. III. Title.
QL737.U56D66 2007
599.638'139—dc22   2006027307

Welcome to the world of wild animals! Meet a young giraffe born on the African savanna. Follow him as he grows up to become the tallest land mammal on Earth!

A newborn giraffe calf stretches his neck to get his first glimpse of the world. His head peeks out from the tall grass.

His mother stands over him to protect him from predators. She licks her calf clean and nudges him to stand up.

Female giraffes are called cows.
Male giraffes are called bulls.
Baby giraffes are called calves.

The calf struggles to get up. He finally stands on his thin, wobbly legs. The newborn giraffe is hungry. He is ready to drink his mother's milk.

Newborn giraffes are about the
same height as an adult human
male. They are about 6 feet
(1.8 meters) tall and weigh about
150 pounds (67.5 kilograms).

Although the young giraffe can stand, he spends much of the first two weeks of life lying down. His mother stands over her calf to protect him from lions and other predators.

The calf grows about 1 inch (2.5 centimeters) taller every day. He is gaining strength.

If a predator comes too close, a giraffe mother kicks it with her front hooves. A kick from a giraffe can seriously injure or kill the predator.

After a few weeks, the calf's mother leaves him with a group of other calves while she eats. Mothers from the herd take turns looking after the calves.

A group of young giraffes
is called a crèche.

11

The young calf is now four months old. He begins eating leaves from trees. He has grown quickly and is now about 9 feet (2.7 m) tall. He is taller than most household ceilings!

When he's not eating, the young giraffe plays, jumps, and runs with the other calves.

Adult giraffes spend more than half of their day eating.

13

At one year old, the calf is old enough to find his own food. He joins his mother to eat from the treetops. Acacia leaves are his favorite.

14

Most giraffes eat about 140 pounds (63 kg) of twigs and leaves per day.

15

When the young giraffe turns three years old, it is time for him to leave his mother and the female herd. He will join other young male giraffes to form a bachelor herd, which is led by an older male.

Female calves stay in their mother's herd. Male calves must leave the female herd.

17

The young giraffe is now five years old. He is living with a bachelor herd. He is 15 feet (4.6 m) tall and weighs 2,800 pounds (1,260 kg).

Many of the other males in the herd are larger and stronger than the young giraffe. He will have to wait until he is older to mate.

Young males stay in their bachelor herds. Older males roam from herd to herd, looking to mate.

19

At 10 years old, the male giraffe is fully grown. It is time for him to fight for the right to mate.

The giraffes swing their heads and necks and slam into each other. The weaker male gives in. The giraffe has proven to the other males that he is strong enough to mate.

Fourteen months after mating with a female, the giraffe becomes a father. This new calf will be the first of many of his calves to grow up on the African savanna.

Fully grown male giraffes stand 18 feet (5.5 m) and weigh about 3,500 pounds (1,575 kg).

Giraffe Diagram

① **EYES** Giraffes can sleep with their eyes open or shut.

② **HORNS** Giraffes are the only animals born with horns.

③ **TONGUE** A giraffe's tongue is about 18 inches (46 cm) long. It uses its tongue to clean its eyes and ears.

④ **NECK** A giraffe's neck is about 6 feet (1.8 m) long. It has the same number of neck bones as a human's neck, but the bones are much larger.

⑤ **SKIN** Giraffes have unique spot patterns on their skin. No two animals' patterns are exactly alike.

⑥ **TAIL** Giraffes have the longest tail of any land mammal.

Map

There is only one species of giraffe, but there are nine different subspecies. They all live in Africa.

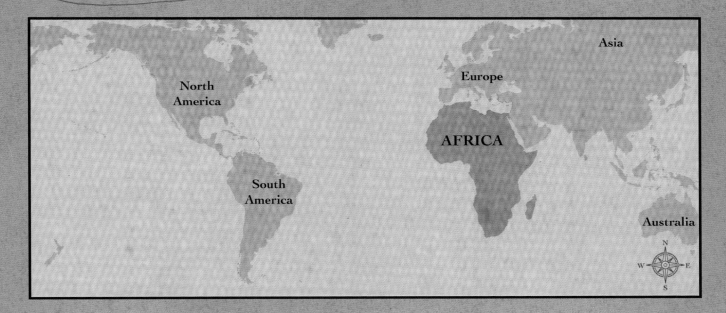

Glossary

acacia—spiny trees or shrubs
bachelor herd—a group of male giraffes
crèche—a group of giraffe calves
herd—a group of animals
mammal—a warm-blooded animal that nurses its young
mate—to join together to produce young
predator—an animal that hunts and eats other animals
savanna—a tropical grassland with few trees

To Learn More

At the Library

Galvin, Laura Gates. *New Baby Giraffe*. Norwalk, Conn.: Soundprints, 2001.
Kalz, Jill. *Giraffes*. North Mankato, Minn.: Creative Education, 2006.
Lockwood, Sophie. *Giraffes*. Chanhassen, Minn.: Child's World, 2005.

On the Web

FactHound offers a safe, fun way to find Web
sites related to this book. All of the sites on
FactHound have been researched by our staff.

1. Visit *www.facthound.com*
2. Type in this special code: 1404831584
3. Click on the FETCH IT button.

Your trusty FactHound will fetch the best sites for you!

Index

drinking, 6
eating, 10, 12, 13, 14
eyes, 22
fighting, 20
herd, 10, 16, 17, 18, 19
horns, 22
mating, 19, 21
neck, 22
playing, 13
predators, 5, 9
savanna, 3, 21
skin, 22
standing, 5, 6, 9
tail, 22
tongue, 22

Look for all of the books in the Wild Animals series:

A Baboon Grows Up

A Crocodile Grows Up

An Elephant Grows Up

A Giraffe Grows Up

A Hippopotamus Grows Up

A Jaguar Grows Up

A Kangaroo Grows Up

A Lion Grows Up

A Rhinoceros Grows Up

A Tiger Grows Up

T2-BWF-056

Plants in Spring

BY M. J. YORK

Published by The Child's World®
1980 Lookout Drive • Mankato, MN 56003-1705
800-599-READ • www.childsworld.com

Photographs ©: iStockphoto, cover, 1; Popular Business/
Shutterstock Images, 4–5; Labrador Photo Video/
Shutterstock Images, 6; Sundraw Photography/
Shutterstock Images, 8–9; Alexander Mazurkevich/
Shutterstock Images, 11; T. M. McCarthy/Shutterstock
Images, 12; Shutterstock Images, 14–15, 16, 18–19;
Mike Laptev/Shutterstock Images, 21

Design Element: Shutterstock Images

ISBN 9781503816541
LCCN 2016945631

Printed in the United States of America
PA02324

ABOUT THE AUTHOR

M. J. York is a writer and editor from Minnesota. She enjoys spring rains and planting her garden.

Contents

CHAPTER 1

Sunshine and Rain...4

CHAPTER 2

Plants Grow...10

CHAPTER 3

Trees in Spring...18

Baking-Cup Flowers Craft...22
Glossary...23
To Learn More...24
Index...24

Sunshine and Rain

It is spring. The days are longer. The sun feels warmer.

4

5

Many plants slept during winter. They wake up in spring. They grow again.

It rains often in spring. Rain helps plants grow.

Plants Grow

New plants begin to **sprout**. Grass grows.

Lawns turn green with thick grass. Rabbits eat the grass.

Soon flowers **bloom**.
Bees and other
insects visit flowers.

We plant seeds in gardens.
Farmers plant their **crops**.

Trees in Spring

Leaves grow on trees. Pine trees grow new needles.

19

Birds build nests in trees.

Spring is here!

Baking-Cup Flowers Craft

Make your own spring flowers!

Supplies:

multicolored baking
cups

scissors

markers or paint
(optional)

green pipe cleaners

Instructions:

1. With your scissors, cut waves or points around the outside of the baking cups to make petals.

2. Decorate the baking cups with markers, paint, or anything you like.

3. Poke a pipe cleaner through the center of each cup. Bend down the end of each pipe cleaner in the middle to hold the cups in place.

Glossary

bloom — (BLOOM) To bloom means to produce flowers. Plants bloom in spring.

crops — (KRAHPS) Crops are plants grown for food. Farmers plant crops in spring.

lawns — (LAWNS) Lawns are areas of grass grown around houses. Lawns turn green again in spring.

sprout — (SPROWT) To sprout means to grow or appear. Grass starts to sprout after spring rains.

To Learn More

Books

Calmenson, Stephanie. *Look! Flowers!*
New York, NY: Little Bee Books, 2016.

Linden, Joanne. *Fiddleheads to Fir Trees: Leaves in All Seasons.* Missoula, MT: Mountain Press Publishing Company, 2013.

Web Sites

Visit our Web site for links about spring plants: **childsworld.com/links**

Note to Parents, Teachers, and Librarians: We routinely verify our Web links to make sure they are safe and active sites. So encourage your readers to check them out!

Index

flowers, 14

grass, 10, 13

leaves, 18

needles, 18
nests, 20

rain, 8

seeds, 17
sun, 4

trees, 18, 20